An American Bird Conservancy Compact Guide

Paul Lehman
Ornithological Editor

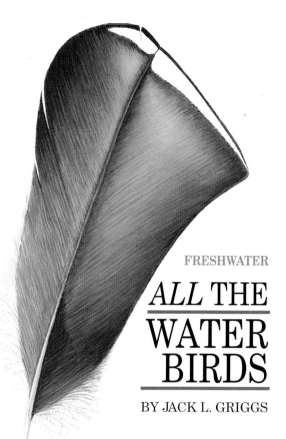

male wood duck

FRESHWATER

ALL THE
WATER
BIRDS

BY JACK L. GRIGGS

HarperPerennial
A Division of HarperCollins*Publishers*

Designed by Jack L. Griggs & Peg Alrich
Edited by Virginia Croft
Illustrations reformatted by John E. Griggs
from the original illustrations published in
All the Birds of North America
by the following artists:

Jonathan Alderfer pp. 29-63, 83-103;
John Dawson p. 105; Hans Peeters pp. 65-81;
Barry Van Dusen pp. 19-27.

HarperCollins books may be purchased for educational, business, or
sales promotional use. For information please write: Special Markets
Department, HarperCollins Publishers, Inc., 10 East 53rd Street, New
York, NY 10022.

FIRST EDITION

Library of Congress Cataloging-in-Publication Data
Griggs, Jack L.
    All the Waterbirds: Freshwater / Jack L. Griggs
        p.   cm.
    Includes index.
    ISBN 0-06-273652-3
1. Water birds—North America—Identification.   I. Title.
QL681.G774 1999
598.176'097—dc21   98-41931
                                                    CIP

99 00 01 02 03 ❖/PE 10 9 8 7 6 5 4 3 2 1

The American Bird Conservancy (ABC) is a U.S.-based, not-for-profit organization formed to unify bird conservation efforts across the Americas and dedicated to the conservation of birds throughout the Western Hemisphere. ABC practices conservation through partnership, bringing together the partners whose expertise and resources are best suited to each task.

The ABC Policy Council has a membership of more than 70 organizations sharing a common interest in the conservation of birds. Composed of ornithologists, policy specialists, educators, and general bird enthusiasts, the Council is a professional forum for exchanging information and discussing critical and emerging bird conservation issues. The Council provides policy and scientific advice to conservationists, stimulates a network of support for conservation policies through national, state, and local groups, and directly accomplishes conservation through ABC.

ABC is a working member of Partners in Flight (PIF), an Americas-wide coalition of more than 150 organizations and government agencies dedicated to bird conservation. Initially begun to find ways to reverse the decline in neotropical migratory bird species, PIF has broadened its scope to include all non-game birds in the Americas. PIF links birders, hunters, government, industry, landowners, and other citizens in a unified effort to conserve bird populations and habitats.

Many North American "birds" found in this guide spend more than half their lives in Latin America and the Caribbean. The needs for bird conservation in this region are at least as great as in the U.S. Through PIF, ABC is building U.S. support for capable, but often underfunded, conservation partners throughout the Americas.

PIF's bird conservation strategy, called the Flight Plan, can be obtained from ABC, the National Fish and Wildlife Foundation, or the U.S. Fish and Wildlife Service. PIF's National Coordinator serves on ABC's staff, and ABC helps implement the Flight Plan through its Important Bird Areas (IBA) initiative. ABC members receive *Bird Conservation*, the magazine about PIF and American bird conservation.

Want to Help Conserve Birds?

It's as Easy as ABC!

By becoming a member of the American
Bird Conservancy, you can help ensure
work is being done to protect many of the
species in this field guide. You can receive *Bird
Conservation* magazine quarterly to learn about bird
conservation throughout the Americas and *World Birdwatch*
magazine for information on international bird conservation.

Make a difference to birds.
Copy this card and mail to the address listed below.

☐ **Yes,** I want to become a member and receive *Bird
Conservation* magazine.
A check in the amount of $18 is enclosed.

☐ **Yes,** I want to become an International member of
ABC and receive both *Bird Conservation* and
World Birdwatch magazines.
A check in the amount of $40 is enclosed.

NAME

ADDRESS

CITY/STATE/ZIP CODE

Return to: American Bird Conservancy
1250 24th Street NW, Suite 400; Washington, DC 20037
or call **1-888-BIRD-MAG** or e-mail: abc@abcbirds.org

Memberships are tax deductible to the extent allowable by law.

CONTENTS

FRESHWATER BIRD HABITAT
Foreword by Edward S. Brinkley 8

IDENTIFYING WATERBIRDS
How to look at a waterbird 15
How to read the maps 16
The birds 17

CHECKLIST AND INDEX 106

FRESH-WATER BIRD HABITAT

by
EDWARD S. BRINKLEY

Water, whether it be running water—a creek, stream, or river—or still water, such as a pond, lake, or reservoir, attracts birds. This is not just because birds come to water to drink (and some do not) but because wetlands produce a vast amount of the foods birds eat: from fish to aquatic insects and crustaceans to aquatic vegetation.

Freshwater wetlands are home to many waterbirds. For them, wetlands are the nurseries in which they raise their young. Even many coastal waterbirds, which otherwise live on salt water, migrate to interior lakes and marshes to nest. Other migrants often use wetlands in the US and southern Canada for stopovers on their way to Arctic nesting sites.

Open water is but one wetland habitat. The margins of open waters—flooded backwaters, grassy marshes, mudflats, or just shrubby vegetation along the water's edge—are wetlands. Lowland bogs, swamps, and marshes characterized more by aquatic vegetation than by open water are wetlands. Habitats on the edges of permanent wetlands (moist woodlands or moist grassy areas) are also wetlands. They depend on some degree of saturation to preserve their particular balance of species.

Birds would argue that rice paddies and flooded farmlands, even wet plowed fields, are wet-

8

lands, although not natural ones. These areas provide the conditions and foods for which waterbirds are especially adapted to forage.

Open water attracts the swimmers—ducks, geese, and others—that we most associate with watery habitats. For most people, fall and winter are the times to see ducks. In the spring and summer, the majority nest from the High Arctic south into the prairie region of central Canada and the northern central US. Some species—mallards, Canada geese, wood ducks, and others—nest south of these sparsely populated regions.

Ducks that feed in deep water are divers. Some chase fish; most feed on bottom vegetation or beds of shellfish. Ducks also use open water to roost (or to take cover in "duck weather"). Loons and cormorants dive for fish in deep water and, when swimming, can be confused with ducks. The Great Lakes and other very large lakes and reservoirs regularly attract oceanic species in small numbers.

**MALLARDS
TIPPING UP**

Closer to the shoreline and in shallow waters, "dabbling" ducks prevail. These ducks pick vegetation and small aquatic animals from the water or the bottom. They are often seen tipping up with only their rears above water as they stretch to reach food on the bottom. The long necks of some waterfowl are special

adult

young

BALD EAGLES

foraging adaptations. Grebes and the white pelican are also found on shallow open water.

Gulls and terns search open water and shorelines for food while in flight. Terns plunge-dive from flight to capture small fish; many also fly over marshy bug-rich areas, capturing flying insects. Gulls are notorious scavengers that can eat almost anything available, so they are found, unlike terns, in great numbers at landfills, as well as in parking lots and farm fields. Many interior gulls prefer nesting on small islands in large lakes, free from animal predators.

Two raptors, the bald eagle and the osprey, also fish over large bodies of fresh water. Both of these birds are recovering from recent disastrous declines and are now increasingly taking up residence near waters with enough fish to support them. Young bald eagles don't have the pure white heads and tails of the adults; their appearance is much more mottled.

Ospreys can be recognized in flight at a good distance. Note how the leading edge of the wing projects forward, gull-like, at the wrist, unlike the wings of the bald eagle or other raptors. The projection is emphasized by the black patch at the wrist contrasting with the white underbody.

OSPREY

Mudflats form on the edges of some bodies of water, whether rivers, lakes, or reservoirs,

10

particularly when water levels are low because of drought. Here shorebirds gather to probe for all the small animal life that lives in the mud. It can be difficult to locate a good mudflat for shorebirds in the interior of the continent. Unlike for waterfowl, there are very few conservation areas that prepare habitat for shorebird migration and nesting.

Many shorebirds are seen in the interior US only in spring and fall as they migrate to and from their Arctic nesting grounds. Others, such as the snipe, killdeer, and spotted sandpiper, nest in suitable habitat over much of the US. Note that the shorebirds' different bill lengths correspond to the different depths of water and mud in which they forage: large shorebirds with long bills, such as the willet, wade in shallow water, whereas small-billed species like the least sandpiper pick at organisms on the water's edge or in bordering dry areas.

UPLAND SANDPIPER

Although sandpipers are a waterbird family, not all sandpipers are true waterbirds. Some species, like the upland sandpiper, are called "grasspipers" for their habit of feeding in dry areas with short grass. Killdeer and buff-breasted sandpipers are equally at home in dry fields or wetlands.

Marshes, bogs, and swamps are areas of heavy vegetation growing in shallow water, either still or slow-moving. Freshwater marshes of the interior are dominated by soft-stemmed grasses such as cattails, bulrushes, and sedges. The plains of the northern US and southern Canada are dotted with sinkhole ponds with extensive marshes. The "potholes" were carved by retreating glaciers and now support one of North America's largest and most important duck nurseries. Grebes use these potholes for nesting too.

Numerous other birds nest or feed in freshwater marshes. Kingfishers sit on perches overhanging water, waiting for fish to appear. Rails, herons, and some shorebirds stalk the water's edges. Terns and swallows feast on the mosquitoes and midges that are often drawn to the air over marshes. And landbirds by the score exploit the resources offered by a healthy marsh. The abundant bird life attracts avian predators, including peregrine falcons and bald eagles.

Bogs are areas of woodland that are flooded or seasonally wet enough to prevent large trees from growing. Often such areas have scattered dead or dying trees. Found mostly in the northeastern US and in Canada, they teem with bird life, though most of the birds are small landbirds or woodpeckers rather than waterbirds. Ducks that nest here are relatively few, as the tannic acid in the water (produced by decaying vegetation) limits the kinds of fish and plants that can live here. Ducks that nest in tree cavities, such as the hooded and common mergansers, often find nesting sites in bogs, though they may forage on rivers and lakes far from their nest holes.

Mergansers, gold-eneyes, buffleheads, and wood ducks nest in large tree cavities. When ready to take to the water, their ducklings catapult out of the hole and into the water, sometimes a drop of 20 feet or more.

Wooded swamps are the southeastern equiv-alent of northern bogs. As in bogs, the slow-moving or still water has a high level of tannin, especially in southern cypress swamps. Wood ducks nest in tree cavities, but few other wa-terbirds nest here. Herons are seen stalking fish, frogs, and other small life, and in some southern swamps, anhingas and wood storks are commonplace. Most of the swamp's birds are landbirds, including barred owls, red-shouldered hawks, swallow-tailed kites, and numerous smaller species.

Cascading mountain streams attract the dipper, a one-of-a-kind bird that somehow feeds in white water that would seem to sweep it away. In the remote mountains of the Northwest, the common and Barrow's gold-eneyes and harlequin duck nest and forage on similar turbulent waters.

MALE HARLEQUIN
DUCK

Among sites that deserve special mention is Florida's Everglades. Although less than one-fifth of this magnificent wetland remains,

13

Some shorebirds and waterfowl use alkaline lakes in the West for feeding during migration, and a few species nest on them.

An alkaline lake has a high pH level (acids create low pH) because of dissolved carbonates and sodium chloride. The high pH restricts the kinds of invertebrates found in alkaline lakes.

Over 60 percent of North America's wetlands have been destroyed since the 1700s. In countless places, local people have watched as a river is dammed, a creek channelized, or a marsh drained—and overnight, species that once nested in abundance are absent.

The collective result is that some species, such as the least tern and the piping plover, which formerly nested in healthy numbers in the continent's interior, are barely hanging on here.

the Everglades National Park is still one of the best places to watch for waterbirds. And it is an excellent place to observe the transition from freshwater to brackish to saltwater habitats.

On the other side of the continent, south-eastern California has the famed Salton Sea. Formed in 1905 when a levee of the Colorado River ruptured, it is now 360 miles square and has a bird list nearing 400 species. This is one of the few places in the interior where one can hope to see oceanic birds that have wandered northward from the Gulf of California. The Salton Sea, like Mono Lake, CA, and Great Salt Lake, UT, is salty; brine shrimp and brine flies abound, attracting huge flocks of migrant birds.

In the center of the continent, the Great Lakes can be a spectacular place to watch birds, particularly in fall when millions of waterbirds migrate through the area, including cormorants, loons, grebes, and all manner of waterfowl. Like the Salton Sea, the Great Lakes attract oceanic species, including migrating jaegers, in fall. Wetlands and wild areas bordering the Great Lakes often attract great numbers of migrating songbirds in spring and fall as well.

It is hoped that visitors to America's fragile wetlands tread lightly and work to protect the health of these invaluable resources.

HOW TO LOOK AT A WATER-BIRD

AERIALISTS

SWIMMERS

WADING BIRDS

SHOREBIRDS

The way birds feed and their adaptations for feeding are the most important points to recognize in identifying and understanding them. For the beginner, the color and pattern of an unknown bird can be so striking that important points of shape and behavior go unnoticed. But feeding adaptations, especially bill shape, best reveal a bird's role in nature—its truest identity.

Waterbirds use one of four general strategies for catching prey. There are aerialists, swimmers, wading birds, and shorebirds. The exceptions are the kingfisher and the dipper. Birds that use the same general strategy resemble one another, and the differences between birds that use different strategies can be recognized at a distance.

The aerialists, such as gulls and terns, fly on long, slender wings, scanning the water and shores below in search of food. The swimmers, such as ducks and cormorants, search for food from the water's surface. The wading birds and shorebirds pursue their prey on foot. Wading birds such as herons stalk through marshes and wetlands. Shorebirds typically probe for small marine organisms on mudflats and beaches. Note that shorebirds often wade, and wading birds can be seen on mudflats and marsh edges with shorebirds.

Young birds, seen in summer and fall, often have a different plumage than adults, but each is the same size and shape as the adult.

HOW TO READ THE MAPS

ange maps provide a simplified picture of a species' distribution. They indicate the birds that can be expected at any locality at different times of the year. Birds are not evenly distributed over their ranges. They require suitable habitat to be present at all and are typically scarcest at their range limits. Some birds are termed "local" because they are found in relatively few specific places and ignore much seemingly suitable habitat.

In spring, many birds migrate north to their nesting territories. In fall, they return south to their wintering grounds. Some birds that nest in the US and Canada winter in Mexico or farther south; a few species migrate thousands of miles to winter at the southern end of South America (where it is summer).

MAP KEY

SUMMER OR NESTING

WINTER

ALL YEAR

MIGRATION
(spring & fall)

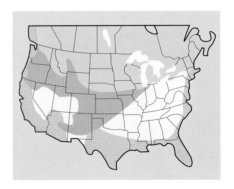

THE BIRDS

Not all ducks are called ducks—teal and scaup, for instance, are also ducks. In the list below, birds with names different from their common group name are listed in parentheses following the group name.

AERIALISTS **18**
gulls, terns

SWIMMERS

LARGER THAN A DUCK **28**
swans, loon, white pelican, anhinga, cormorant, geese

DUCK-SIZED **38**
ducks (mallard, gadwall, pintail, shoveler, wigeon, teal, scaup, redhead, canvasback, goldeneye, bufflehead, mergansers), grebes, gallinule, moorhen, coot

WADING BIRDS

HERON-SIZED **64**
crane, herons (egrets, bittern, night-herons), ibises, limpkin

RAIL-SIZED **78**
rails (sora)

SHOREBIRDS

LARGE SHOREBIRDS **82**
stilt, avocet, large sandpipers (curlew, whimbrel, godwit)

MEDIUM SHOREBIRDS **86**
medium sandpipers (yellowlegs, willet, dowitchers, turnstone, snipe, medium plovers (killdeer)

SMALL SHOREBIRDS **94**
small plovers, small sandpipers (dunlin, phalarope)

DIPPER AND KINGFISHER **104**

17

HERRING GULL

CALIFORNIA GULL

The red spot on the bill seen on many adult gulls is thought to be a pecking target for nestlings demanding food.

There are three white-headed gulls that can be confused with one another, the herring and California in this illustration and the ring-billed in the next. All are numerous. The herring and ring-billed are widespread and can be seen almost anywhere during migration.

Herring gulls are the largest of the three. Don't be confused by the herring gull being about the same size as the California in the illustration. It is shown at a bit of an angle, foreshortened. The same illusions happen in real life bird-watching. Size can be an uncertain mark.

Better marks for separating adult **California** and **herring** gulls are mantle color, leg color, and the shape and color of the bill. Mantle color is the best mark at a distance. The California gull's mantle is a noticeable shade darker than the herring's or the ring-bill's. Its legs are greenish yellow or gray, never pink as in the herring gull. The bill is more slender in the California gull and has a black mark as well as a red spot, although a very few herring gulls can show a black mark, too.

California gulls are also distinguished by their dark eyes and the white crescent seen just below mid-back on a standing bird. Known as the scapular crescent, it is thin or lacking in the other white-headed gulls.

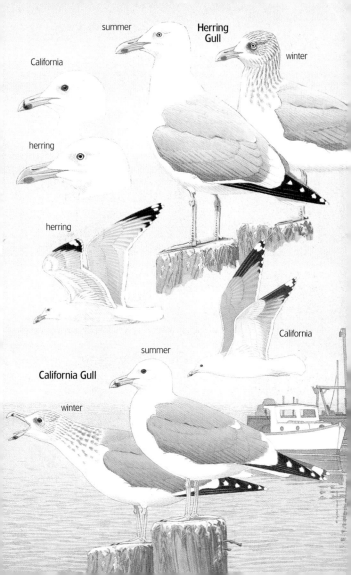

summer

Herring
Gull

California

herring

winter

herring

California

California Gull

summer

winter

FRANKLIN'S GULL

BONAPARTE'S GULL

RING-BILLED GULL

Both Franklin's and Bonaparte's may show a pink blush on their breasts in fresh spring plumage. It soon fades.

Ring-billed gulls are abundant and increasing. The birds have adapted to agricultural lands and urban areas, where they scavenge or take insects, worms, and grain. They aren't likely to be confused with the smaller, black-headed gulls in this illustration, but they resemble the herring and California gulls shown on the preceding page.

The **ring-billed gull** is the smallest of the three white-headed gulls, about two-thirds the size of the herring gull. The distinct black ring on the yellow bill is the easiest mark. Note that all the white-headed gulls have brownish gray streaks on their heads and necks in winter.

Franklin's gull is a familiar bird of prairie marshes in migration and summer. Flocks also scour freshly plowed fields for worms and insects. Bonaparte's gull is more widespread and occurs in the US in winter and during migration.

Franklin's gull is larger and darker-backed than **Bonaparte's.** Franklin's thicker bill, blood red in summer, is a sure mark. Bonaparte's bill is slender and black. In fall migration, Franklin's retains about half of its hood—enough that the white eye crescents remain obvious.

In flight, the two gulls display distinctively different black-and-white wing tip patterns. Also note the gray down the middle of Franklin's tail.

20

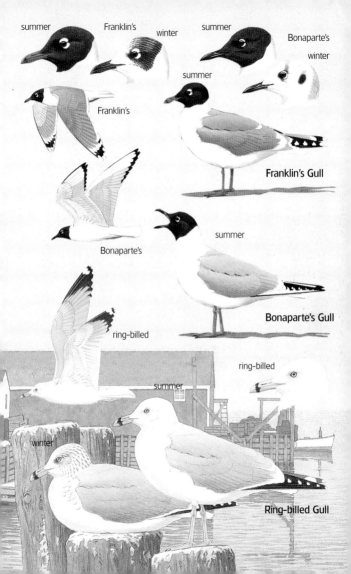

summer   Franklin's   winter   summer   Bonaparte's

winter

Franklin's   summer

Franklin's Gull

Bonaparte's   summer

Bonaparte's Gull

ring-billed

ring-billed

summer

winter

Ring-billed Gull

When the other waterbirds have been identified, try your hand at the young brown gulls. All the brownish gulls with a dark band on their tails are young birds.

It takes four years in the larger gull species for a young bird to attain the smooth gray-and-white plumage of an adult. During those years, youngsters molt into several different brown-and-gray variations. The youngest birds (in their first-winter plumage) are the darkest and are the birds illustrated standing. The color lightens after molting each spring and fall until adult plumage is achieved. Gray begins to show on a large gull's back in the second summer.

Typically there will be as many or more young gulls (one to three years old) on a beach as there are mature gulls, which can live 20 years or more. And perhaps half the young birds will be in their first year. The proportions of the age groups reveal the story of early mortality in gulls.

Young birds are the same size as adults, and size is a good clue in a mixed flock. First identify the adults, then match the brown gulls with the adults by size when possible. Next, check the bill size and shape. Bill shape is the same in young birds as it is in adults.

The bill and legs are also good marks, although they aren't necessarily the same color as those of the adult. Note particularly on the young herring gull how the black tip of the bill blends to a pale base. In their second winter, a young herring gull's bill shows a black ring similar to that seen on adult ring-billed gulls.

22

1st winter

1st summer

Bonaparte's Gull

Franklin's Gull

1st summer

2nd summer

Ring-billed Gull

2nd summer

3rd winter

California Gull

2nd winter

3rd winter

Herring Gull

CASPIAN TERN

LEAST TERN

BLACK TERN

Terns that have been displaced from beaches, like the least tern and the Caspian, now attempt to nest on substitute sites. The most successful substitutes have been dredge-spoil islands.

Terns look different than gulls, more slender and streamlined, with pointed bills, long pointed wings, and forked tails. They behave differently too. They don't glide as gulls often do but cruise along on continuous wing strokes. Some terns plunge-dive for fish; gulls normally don't. Other terns pluck their meals from the clouds of insects over marshes in summer. Most terns both fish and take insects.

Least terns are the smallest, scarcest, and most endangered of the freshwater terns. They prefer to nest on sand bars or beaches and have been displaced from most such sites by people.

The least tern is usually seen flying alone over shallow water, bill pointed down as it searches for fish. It often hovers before plunging. The small size is one good mark for the **least tern;** the yellow bill with the black tip is the clincher. Also note the patch of white on the forehead.

Black terns are marsh dwellers that prefer taking insects. They are most numerous in the West. **Black terns** are obvious in summer plumage, but during migration many are molting and have a patchy appearance.

Its bulky body and heavy red bill distinguish the **Caspian tern** in all seasons. The black cap is streaked with white in winter. It is fairly numerous on lakeshores in summer and migration.

24

young

Caspian Tern

summer

Caspian

black

summer

winter

least

black

least

young

young

summer

summer

Least Tern

Black Tern

COMMON TERN

FORSTER'S TERN

The eggs and hatchlings in colonies of nesting terns are the natural prey of some large gulls. These gulls have adapted well to humans and their garbage, and populations of such species as herring and ring-billed gulls have greatly increased. Terns populations, as a result, have suffered.

Both Forster's and the common tern are numerous in summer and during migration. In winter, only Forster's terns remain in the US, and nearly all are on coasts.

Forster's and common terns can be difficult to separate, even with binoculars. One of the first clues is habitat. **Forster's** prefers marshes, where it preys on large flying insects more often than on fish. The **common tern** prefers plunge-diving for fish along lakeshores and in rivers. However, both species are comfortable behaving like the other.

Bill color in summer is also helpful but not a certain clue. The bill is typically more orange in Forster's, deeper red in the common tern. Individuals with black bills in spring are yearlings; they also lack a full cap. By late summer, the brightly colored bills of adults begin turning black and the birds begin losing their black caps. At the same time, the common tern develops a distinctive dark shoulder bar. Shoulder bars are also good marks for young common terns.

In flight, the outer surface of the upper wing is a good mark. It is paler than the mantle (frosted looking, some say) in Forster's, darker than the mantle in the common. When Forster's stands, its long forked tail extends beyond the folded wing tip and is a certain mark.

26

common

Forster's

summer

summer

winter

winter

common
(late summer)

Forster's

summer

Common Tern

young

winter

young

summer

Forster's Tern

winter

TRUMPETER SWAN

TUNDRA SWAN

MUTE SWAN

The trumpeter swan has been the object of conservation efforts since the 1930s, when hunting reduced their known population to 69 birds. Their recovery has been slow and steady.

None of the swans are seen over most of North America. Tundra swans are the most numerous (about 150,000 birds), but they nest in the Arctic, winter in flocks at a relatively few, mostly coastal sites, and stop in migration only at traditional staging areas.

Trumpeter swans are scarcer than tundra swans and also distributed very locally. Numerous restoration projects are reintroducing trumpeter flocks at sites throughout the bird's historical range, especally in the Midwest.

Wild mute swans have become fairly numerous in certain localities in the Northeast and around the Great Lakes. The swan of European fairy tales, it was introduced in North America to decorate parks and estates, swimming with its neck gracefully curved and its wings partially flared. Now established in the wild, mute swans have become dangerous pests in some areas because of their size and aggressiveness.

The orange bill with a black knob is a certain mark for the **mute swan.** Bills are also the best marks separating the **tundra** from the larger **trumpeter swan,** but the differences are subtle. Tundra swans usually have a spot of yellow before the eye. Trumpeter swans have larger bills with a straighter ridge, and their eye is more enclosed in the black facial skin.

28

trumpeter

tundra

tundra

Tundra Swan

Mute Swan

COMMON LOON

WHITE PELICAN

With loons disappearing from the northern tier of states in the 1970s, Loon Watch programs were established in many localities. Volunteer Loon Rangers have guarded nests, improved habitat, and conducted education programs. Populations are recovering.

The haunting calls of the common loon have become the symbolic sounds of the wilderness. The yodeling, wailing, and maniacal laughter carries for miles around the northern lakes where loons nest. Most winter on salt water, but some take their time reaching the coast. Individuals can be seen on northern lakes and reservoirs until just before freeze-up.

Exquisitely patterned birds, loons are a favorite subject of artists and photographers. Field marks are not needed. Even at a distance, the distinctive shape of the **common loon** on the water can be recognized. Loons spend almost their entire lives on water, diving for small fish.

Field marks don't need to be remembered for **white pelicans** either. Anybody encountering one for the first time would probably say, "Look, a white pelican!" In spring, they grow an ornamental plate on the bill. By summer, the plate is shed and the head turns grayish.

White pelicans don't plunge-dive like brown pelicans. They swim and use their bills like nets to scoop up small fish in shallow waters. It's hard to sneak up on fish, even little ones, when you are the size of a pelican. They solve that problem by fishing together. Through co-ordinated movements, they herd small schooling fish toward each other or into shore.

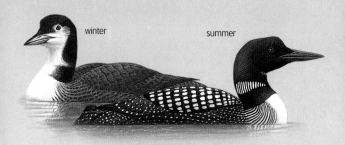

winter summer

Common Loon

White Pelican

ANHINGA AND CORMORANT

ANHINGA

DOUBLE-CRESTED CORMORANT

The neotropic cormorant is fairly numerous in southern and coastal Texas and Louisiana. There are also a few in southern Arizona. The neotropic is noticeably smaller than the double-crested and has a proportionally longer tail. The throat pouch is dull yellow with a narrow, sharply angled, white border in adults.

The **anhinga's** pointed yellow bill and snake-like head and neck are often all that is visible as the bird swims, body submerged. It dives frequently, searching for fish to spear with its lethally sharp bill. After fishing, anhingas find a limb or other perch and spread their wings to dry, as cormorants do. Curiously, small groups of anhingas enjoy soaring high in the sky, like hawks or vultures. Their long necks and tails give them a distinctive look when soaring, like tiny crosses.

Anhingas are fairly numerous in swamps and ponds in their restricted southern range. Males have silver plumes on their wings; females and young, a tawny neck and breast.

The **double-crested cormorant's** bill is hooked to catch fish, not spear them like the anhinga. The orange-yellow throat skin is a flexible pouch that expands to hold the catch. In flight, double-crested cormorants kink their necks distinctively. They are numerous inland in summer and during migration.

The feathers on most diving birds are structured so that they are waterproof, but the cormorant and anhinga must hang their wings out to dry because the outer layer of their plumage is wetable. An inner layer is waterproof and helps keep the bird warm in cold water.

Anhinga

♀

♂

western form
early summer

young

eastern form

Double-crested
Cormorant

WHITE-FRONTED GOOSE

CANADA GOOSE

A darker race of the white-fronted, the tule goose winters in the Sacramento Valley, CA, and stops over at Oregon's Klamath Basin during migration.

In the eastern states, the white-fronted goose is a rare but increasingly frequent visitor.

White-fronted geese are grazers that have adapted to agricultural fields, where they now feed on waste grains in winter. They usually roost in flocks on water but sometimes settle for bare ground. Migration is widespread, with large numbers gathering at a few staging areas, such as central Nebraska and the Klamath Basin of southern Oregon.

Our only gray-brown goose, the white-fronted most closely resembles the domestic gray goose. The name refers to the small white band above the bill. A better mark for the adult **white-fronted goose** is the dark speckled belly. Legs are usually orange; the bill is usually pink, but these colors vary. Flocks fly in Vs and give a high-pitched, two-noted, "laughing" call.

Canada geese are grazers also. In parts of the East, golf courses and other grassy areas attract flocks that now stay year-round and have become pests.

The black stocking–like head and neck of the **Canada goose** and the white chin strap are familiar throughout the continent. Even flocks in flight are recognized by the V-formation flight and resounding honks. There are many races, some barely larger than a mallard and weighing as little as 3 pounds, others three feet long and weighing 15 pounds.

domestic gray goose

White-fronted Goose

young

Canada Goose

medium-sized race with white neck ring

large race

small race "cackling goose"

Ross' goose was headed for extinction in the mid-1900s from hunting pressure and loss of habitat. It has since rebounded with reduced hunting pressure and by adapting to agricultural lands for grazing.

There are three varieties of white geese in North America. Ross' goose is considered a species. The other two, the greater snow goose and the lesser snow goose, are considered races of the snow goose.

The greater snow goose winters in the East, most on salt water. Lesser snow geese (only slightly smaller than the greater) winter in western and central states. Most flocks of Ross' winter in California's Central Valley, but they are increasing in the central states.

All three geese winter in flocks in shallow wetlands but often feed in nearby agricultural fields (which were often wetlands providing natural foods before being drained for agriculture). They fly in distinctive wavy lines.

There are other large white birds with black wing tips, including the white pelican (p. 30), but they don't look like geese. The white on the head and breast is often rust-stained on snow geese, rarely so on Ross' goose.

Lesser snow geese have a common "blue" form (illustrated in flight) rarely seen in greater snow geese or Ross' geese. **Ross' goose** is noticeably smaller than **snow geese** and has a stubbier bill that lacks the "grinning patch" of snow geese. Inconspicuous "warts" develop at the base of Ross' bill with age.

36

domestic white goose

Ross'

snow

Ross'

blue goose form of snow goose

snow

young

Ross' Goose

Snow Goose

FULVOUS WHISTLING-DUCK

WOOD DUCK

Black-bellied whistling ducks are a tropical species that is resident in southern Texas. A few reach southern Arizona in summer. Shaped like the fulvous whistling-duck, they have a black belly, a bright red bill, and a white wing patch.

Whistling-ducks are scarce, even in their limited range. Their nocturnal habits make them even harder to see. Usually in small flocks, they now feed heavily in rice fields, mostly at night. They also occupy their original habitat, marshes with thick vegetation.

The long neck and legs of the **fulvous whistling-duck** give it a distinctive goose-like appearance. The name refers to the tawny head, neck, and sides. The white rump and side stripe are also useful marks.

Wood ducks are much easier to find than whistling-ducks. Wood ducks occupy wooded streams, ponds, and swamps, where they nest in tree cavities or in nest boxes set out for them. It was once feared they would follow two other birds of wooded swamplands, the Carolina parakeet and ivory-billed woodpecker, to extinction. However, they have proven resilient and have recovered from overhunting to reoccupy their original range.

The male **wood duck,** with his gaudy plumage and red eyes and bill, is easily identified. Females are much duller but have a distinctive tear-shaped white eye mark. Female mandarin ducks, a non-native species sometimes found in park ponds, look like female wood ducks but have a narrower eye-ring.

38

Fulvous Whistling-duck

♂

♀

Wood Duck

BLACK DUCK

MOTTLED DUCK

MALLARD

The brightly colored wing patch is known as the speculum and is a useful mark. It is bright blue with white borders in the mallard, purple in the black duck, and slightly greenish in the mottled duck

allards and their close relatives, black ducks and mottled ducks, won't be seen on deep water. They are not diving ducks but dabblers—ducks that feed from the surface or tip up to feed on bottom vegetation.

Nothing looks like a male **mallard,** although the male shoveler (p. 44) has a green head. However, many ducks resemble the mottled-brown female, especialy the female gadwall (p. 42). The mallard's best marks are her bill, tail, and feather pattern. The bill is orange with a black saddle mark on top, the tail shows white, and the body feathers are truly mottled.

Black ducks hybridize with mallards and are gradually disappearing as a species. **Black ducks** are darker than female mallards (male darkest). A good mark is the dark tail. Males have yellow bills; females, yellow-green with some black flecking. Note that the body feathers have buff edges but no interior mottling.

Of the three mallard-like species, only mottled ducks are seen (in the wild) along the Gulf Coast and Florida in summer. The **mottled duck** has a dark tail and yellow bill (dark flecking on the female's). Note the contrast of the dark body with the pale unstreaked throat and cheek. Mottled ducks hybridize with feral mallards, producing intermediates.

Black Duck

black

♂

♀

Mottled Duck

mottled

mallard

♂

Mallard

♀

downy young

GADWALL

PINTAIL

The gadwall was a western duck in the early 1900s. Since then it has expanded its range to the East Coast and has been introduced in many eastern states. The eastern population continues to grow.

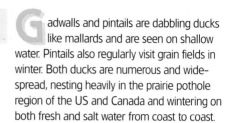

adwalls and pintails are dabbling ducks like mallards and are seen on shallow water. Pintails also regularly visit grain fields in winter. Both ducks are numerous and widespread, nesting heavily in the prairie pothole region of the US and Canada and wintering on both fresh and salt water from coast to coast.

Gadwalls are usually seen in small flocks, often with pintails. The male **gadwall** is a dull gray-brown. His only good plumage marks are the black under the tail and the white speculum. Female gadwalls also have the distinctive white speculum. The female suggests a female mallard, but note the dark tail, steeper forehead, and gray bill with orange edges.

The **pintail** is one of the most abundant North American ducks. It would be hard to mistake the elegant male. The female has the same slender shape as the male, but her plumage resembles that of other brown female ducks. The white belly is a useful mark, but the longish bill, rounded head, and long, slender neck are the best marks.

The profile of the neck, head, and bill is a reliable mark for many ducks. Note especially the angle formed where the bill joins the forehead. It is a continuous slope in the pintail, a fairly steep angle in the gadwall.

pintail

gadwall

♂ Gadwall

♀

Pintail

♂ ♀

SHOVELER

AMERICAN WIGEON

Rarely in a flock of American wigeons it is possible to see a Eurasian wigeon. The male Eurasian wigeon has a red-brown head and a buff crown; its sides are gray. Females are very much like American wigeons but have slightly warmer colored heads.

Wigeons and shovelers are most numerous in the West, but they are fairly common in the East as well. They are dabblers, found in shallow water, although wigeons are commonly seen grazing on short grass, such as on golf courses.

The male **shoveler's** colors suggest a male mallard, and the female has plumage very much like the female mallard's. However, the outsized bill and long, sloping forehead give the shoveler—male and female—a distinctive look. Males have black bills (not yellow as in the mallard); females have an orange edge to their dusky bills. In flight, shovelers show green speculums and blue wing patches like the teal to which they are closely related.

The shoveler's bill is specialized for straining tiny aquatic animals from the water, and the bird is often seen swimming low in the water with its bill, even its head, submerged. Shovelers often feed in small groups in winter.

The **American wigeon** has a fairly steep forehead and a stubby bluish bill with a black tip. Males are bright and distinctive; females, reddish brown with a grayish head. Note the green speculum and white shoulder patch (grayish in females) in flight. They fly swiftly in compact, noisy, agile flocks.

44

Shoveler

young ♂

♀

♂

shoveler

wigeon

American Wigeon

♀

♂

CINNAMON TEAL

BLUE-WINGED TEAL

GREEN-WINGED TEAL

Teal and most ducks molt all their flight feathers at once a few weeks after nesting. At this time the birds are especially vulnerable. Males wear a concealing "eclipse" plumage resembling the female's.

eal are the smallest dabbling ducks. They often feed in small groups, dabbling for seeds and other tiny plants and animals in the shallow water stirred up by their swimming. Green-winged teal are the most abundant. Blue-winged teal are numerous in summer, but most of them winter south of the US. West of the Rockies, cinnamon teal are numerous in summer.

Like most dabbling ducks, male **teal** are bright and distinctive. It is the females that can cause identification problems. They look much alike when seen swimming—small and mottled brown, with dark bills. However, females usually associate with males of the same species.

The best confirming marks for a female are the size of the bill and the color of the forewing. Bills come in three sizes; small (green-winged), medium (blue-winged), and large (cinnamon).

The green-winged is the only teal without blue forewings. (Also note the rusty border to the female's green speculum.) The remaining teal and the shoveler (p. 44) have distinctive blue forewings that distinguish them from all other ducks. Female blue-wings are grayer than the brownish female cinnamon teal. Note the distinct dark eye line and the pale spot at the base of the female blue-wing's bill.

Cinnamon Teal

♂

♀

cinnamon

blue-winged

Blue-winged Teal

♀

♂

green-winged

Green-winged Teal

♀

♂

LESSER SCAUP

RING-NECKED DUCK

Greater scaup are numerous along the Atlantic and Pacific coasts in winter. They closely resemble lesser scaup but have rounder heads and slightly larger bills with a larger "nail" at the tip. In flight, the wing stripe is white almost to the tip of the wing.

esser scaup and ring-necked ducks dive to feed on bottom vegetation and aquatic life such as shellfish. They can dive 40 feet but usually feed in shallower water. In very shallow water, they tip up like dabblers. They are numerous on fresh water in summer and during migration and remain fairly numerous in winter, although many migrate south of the US. Scaup often form large flocks ("rafts") on deep water.

Male **lesser scaup, ring-necks,** and redheads (next illustration) all have similar shapes and plumage patterns. There is also a greater scaup, a coastal bird (see sidebar), with the same look. Head color distinguishes the male redhead, and the white ring on the bill is a good mark for the male ring-neck. Better marks for male ring-necks at a distance are the vertical white stripe on the side before the wing and the black back. Scaup and redheads have gray backs.

Female scaup, ring-necks, and redheads are more alike than the males. Female redheads don't have the white around the bill seen on the other two females, although there is often a pale area. Note the thin white eye-ring and line behind the eye in the female ring-neck. In flight, ring-necks show a gray wing stripe, lesser scaup have a white stripe that turns gray at the tip of the wing, and redheads have no wing stripe.

48

♂ ♀

Lesser Scaup

scaup

Ring-necked Duck

scaup taking off

♀

♂

REDHEAD

CANVASBACK

RUDDY DUCK

Most diving ducks propel themselves underwater with their webbed feet. For efficient diving, the legs are placed well back on the body, so far back that some, like the ruddy duck, struggle to walk on land.

edheads, canvasbacks, and ruddy ducks are divers that feed primarily on bottom vegetation. They all nest in freshwater marshes and migrate in small groups to large lakes or coastal bays for winter. Sometimes the redhead is seen in shallow water with dabblers.

Ruddy ducks usually stay to themselves in small groups throughout the winter. Redheads and canvasbacks often gather in large mixed flocks.

Redheads are shaped like the scaup and ring-necked duck shown on the preceding page and are closely related. Female redheads are a tawnier brown than scaup and don't show white at the base of the bill, although the area may be pale.

The male canvasback has a black breast and a chestnut head and neck like the redhead, but its back and sides are nearly white compared to the gray-bodied redhead. Best mark for the **canvasback**—especially the female—is the long, slightly dished bill and forehead.

Their stiff tails and thick necks give the smaller **ruddy ducks** an unusual look. The tail is often cocked at a 45-degree angle. For males, the white cheeks are good marks in summer and winter. Winter males lack the bright blue bill so prominent on summer males. Females have gray cheeks divided by a darker brown line.

50

redhead

canvasback

Redhead

♀

♂

Canvasback

♀

♂

Ruddy Duck

winter ♂

summer ♂

♂

**COMMON
GOLDENEYE**

**BARROW'S
GOLDENEYE**

Ducks that nest in cavities—the goldeneyes, bufflehead, wood duck, and hooded and common mergansers—tend to dump eggs into each other's nests. Take a close look at the downy young of cavity-nesting ducks to see if they are all the same species.

oldeneyes are diving ducks. In winter, they gather on large lakes, rivers, and coastal bays and feed primarily on shellfish. In summer, they live on woodland lakes and streams, where they nest in tree cavities or nest boxes set out for them. Their summer diet is more varied and includes insects.

The common goldeneye is fairly numerous, much more so than Barrow's goldeneye. Barrow's is especially scarce south of Canada. Goldeneyes are seldom seen in large flocks, usually migrating and foraging in small groups.

Goldeneyes have puffy heads, which they often hold low so that the dark head and back look continuous. When the head is held erect, the white neck can be seen. The head sheen is green in the male common, purple in the male Barrow's, but under field conditions, the heads often appear flat black. The sure mark for the male **common goldeneye** is the white spot before the eye. The male **Barrow's goldeneye** has a white crescent and a dark shoulder bar.

Both females have brown heads, narrow white collars, and bright yellow eyes. They are best distinguished by head and bill shape; note the steep forehead and stubby, triangular bill of Barrow's. In flight, goldeneyes produce a whistling sound that is one of their best marks.

♀ ♂ **Common Goldeneye**

Barrow's   common

♂ ♀ **Barrow's Goldeneye**

HOODED MERGANSER

BUFFLEHEAD

Harlequin ducks nest along rushing mountain streams in the Pacific Northwest, where they feed agilely in the cascading torrents.

Male harlequins are dark, with a handful of oddly placed and shaped white marks. Females are dull and dark, with two or three small white marks on the face.

Buffleheads and hooded mergansers are small diving ducks, small enough to spring directly into flight. (Most diving ducks are so heavy they must run across the water flapping furiously in order to get their bulk airborne.) They are fairly numerous, especially around the Great Lakes.

Buffleheads feed and behave much like their close relatives, the goldeneyes (p. 52), but do so more actively. Note the puffy head that inspired the **bufflehead's** name. The steep forehead and short bill are also helpful marks. For males, the large white head patch is an easy mark. Females are more drab overall but have a distinctive small white cheek patch.

Like buffleheads, hooded mergansers nest in cavities and live on forested lakes and streams. They dive for fish, crayfish, insects, and the like and are usually seen singly or in small flocks.

The crest is a good mark for the **hooded merganser.** The female's is a bushy gray-brown. Males have a dramatic black-and-white crest, which they can raise and lower. When lowered, the white fan-shaped mark becomes a white line behind the eye. Young birds are like females but show less crest. Note the distinctive narrow bill, which marks the difference between mergansers and other ducks.

54

♀ ♂

Hooded Merganser

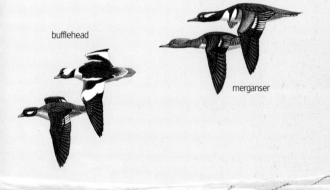

bufflehead

merganser

♀ ♂

Bufflehead

RED-BREASTED MERGANSER

COMMON MERGANSER

Mergansers sometimes sink slowly beneath the water like a grebe. They do it by releasing air captured in their feathers and by expelling air from internal air sacs. They more commonly dive with a quick forward flip.

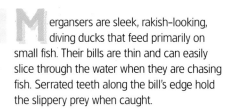

Mergansers are sleek, rakish-looking, diving ducks that feed primarily on small fish. Their bills are thin and can easily slice through the water when they are chasing fish. Serrated teeth along the bill's edge hold the slippery prey when caught.

The red-breasted merganser is numerous but seen only during migration inland in the US, usually in small groups on lakes and rivers. The Great Lakes are as far south as they nest; most winter along coasts. Common mergansers live year-round on fresh water. They winter as far north as water stays open, sometimes forming large flocks on lakes and rivers.

The **common merganser** is the largest of all the North American inland ducks. Males are mostly white with a dark green head and red bill; they don't show the obvious crest that characterizes the red-breasted merganser. **Red-breasted mergansers** have a thinner bill, steeper forehead, and red eyes; males show the namesake red(dish) breast at the waterline. The best mark for separating female common and red-breasted mergansers is the clean line between the neck and breast in the common.

Mergansers fly close to the water except in migration. The white speculum of the red-breasted has distinctive dark bars on it.

♀

♂

molting young ♂

Red-breasted Merganser

red-breasted

common

Common Merganser

♂

♀

GREBES

PIED-BILLED GREBE

**CLARK'S AND
WESTERN GREBES**

Clark's and western grebes have long been considered forms of a single species because bill color and face pattern are only slightly different and because they are often seen in mixed groups behaving identically. However, the birds apparently recognize their slight differences in appearance and calls and prefer mating with their own kind.

Grebes look something like ducks, but the families are not closely related. They are almost always seen on the water, as they rarely fly except in migration and never come ashore. Nests are built in marshy vegetation. When startled, they rapidly dive. Hell-diver is one of their common names. They dive for food—small fish, tiny shellfish, aquatic insects—and also pick morsels from the water's surface.

The pied-billed grebe is numerous in marshes. Unlike other grebes, it often submerges only partially; the head remains above water to keep an eye on the situation. Nothing more is needed for identification. The gray-brown head and short, chicken-like bill of the **pied-billed grebe** can only be confused with the coot (p. 62), which is darker and has red eyes.

Clark's and western grebes are numerous in summer and during migration on open fresh water with marshy borders, where they engage in spectacular and varied courtship rituals. They winter on coasts or large lakes. **Clark's grebe** has the more orange bill, and its eye is surrounded by white, not black or gray, as in the **western grebe.** Not all birds are easy to separate into one species or another, but the males of both species can often be separated from the females, which have noticeably thinner and shorter bills.

Pied-billed Grebe

young

downy chicks

Clark's Grebe

typical

Western Grebe

pale

GREBES

EARED GREBE

HORNED GREBE

RED-NECKED GREBE

Grebes don't have webs between their toes like ducks. Instead, their toes have broad lobes to help with swimming.

Grebes summer on open bodies of fresh water with marshy edges. They nest in the concealing marsh grasses and fish in the open waters. The northern nesting range of the red-necked and horned grebes barely extends into southern Canada and the US, but eared grebes nest over a large portion of the western US and are numerous. Some horned grebes and eared grebes remain inland over the winter; the others head for the coasts.

Eared, horned, and **red-necked grebes** have a similar look in summer, but they also have distinctive features. The eared grebe has a black neck and head with a spray of golden feathers behind the eye. On the horned grebe, the golden tuft surrounds the eye and extends back in a line. Both horned and red-necked grebes have a red neck. The sure marks for the red-necked are the white cheek and chin.

In winter, eared and horned grebes look similar, patterned in shades of black and white. Eared grebes are darker, with black on the cheek extending well below the eye. The thin, slightly upturned bill and steep, pointy forehead are even better marks. The horned grebe has a crisp neck pattern similar to that of the much larger western grebe shown on the preceding page; its head is flatter and bill heavier than those of the eared grebe.

60

summer winter **Eared Grebe**

winter summer **Horned Grebe**

Red-necked Grebe

young summer winter

COOTS AND ALLIES

PURPLE GALLINULE

MOORHEN

COOT

Coots, moorhens, and gallinules all pump their heads distinctively as they swim, a mark that can be seen at a good distance.

Coots and their close relatives the purple gallinule and moorhen are more closely related to rails (p. 80) than to ducks. Like rails, they sometimes wade in marshes and have large feet for walking on floating marsh vegetation. However, they frequently use their feet to swim like a duck. Coots even have lobed toes like the grebes for efficient swimming.

Coots are abundant, except in the Northeast, and fairly tame. They are very resourceful and can eke out a living on an oversized puddle. They feed from the surface and by diving, taking plant and animal life. The **coot** is a slate black bird with a distinctive chicken-like bill that extends up the forehead as a shield. The shield has a dark red spot, and the ivory bill has a dark band near the tip that suggests the bill of the pied-billed grebe (p. 58).

The **moorhen** is dark like a coot but has a thin white side stripe. The adult sports a bright red shield and bill with a yellow tip. Moorhens are warier than coots.

Purple gallinules are the wariest of the three and the scarcest, even in their limited range. They spend as much time wading in cover as swimming. There isn't much chance of misidentifying adult **purple gallinules.** Young birds are tawnier than young coots or moorhens.

young

Purple Gallinule

young

Moorhen

young

Coot

downy chicks

SANDHILL CRANE

ranes are famous for the stunning leaps and gyrations of their courtship dancing. The sheer size of the sandhill is impressive, even when it is seen standing still or flying overhead. Sandhills feed on just about anything edible that comes their way—small animals, large insects, seeds, berries. Grain from agricultural fields has become a major food item during migration and winter, and birds are seen on stubble fields and dry prairies as often as on freshwater marshes.

Because of their similar sizes, **sandhill cranes** are sometimes confused with the great blue heron in the next illustration. Cranes are grayer (sometimes stained with iron oxide), have a naked red forehead, and fly with their necks extended, not folded as in the great blue. They are noisy birds, often heard before they are seen. Their resonant bugling can carry a mile. Family units gather into large groups during migration and at some wintering sites.

There are small resident populations of sandhills in Florida and Mississippi. Only about 100 birds remain in Mississippi, and most of them were captive-raised.

Florida's resident population of 4,000 to 5,000 sandhills is increased six-fold in winter by migrating birds that nest primarily around the Great Lakes.

Most sandhills migrate. They stage (gather before or during migration) at a relatively few traditional sites. The majority stage in spring in the Platte River Valley, Nebraska, and winter at a score of lakes in west Texas and along the Gulf Coast. A smaller eastern population winters in Florida and migrates through the Pulaski Fish and Wildlife Area in northwestern Indiana.

64

young

Sandhill Crane

DARK HERONS

GREAT BLUE HERON

LITTLE BLUE HERON

The tricolored heron is primarily a saltwater heron that also feeds in fresh water near the Atlantic and Gulf coasts and throughout Florida. About the size of a little blue heron, the tricolored is the only slender heron with a contrasting white belly.

Great blue herons are widespread and numerous. Most retreat from northern wetlands in winter, but some stay until marshes freeze. Great blues prefer to feed in marshes but are versatile in where they feed and what they eat. Fish is their favorite prey. They typically hunt alone, wading slowly or waiting patiently. With a rapid thrust of its bill, the great blue spears prey that ventures too close.

Great blue herons may be confused with the sandhill crane shown on the preceding page. Great blues have neck stripes and black head plumes. A good mark is the shape of the neck. A crane's neck curves gently; a heron's has a kink except when fully extended. Herons fly with folded necks. The illustration shows a great blue taking off, in the process of folding its neck.

The little blue is the smaller of the two dark herons seen on fresh water. Like the great blue, it usually fishes alone, slowly. Though numerous, little blues are often inconspicuous in shadows.

Little blue herons are so much smaller than great blue herons that, in this case, size is a very reliable field mark. Often the little blue appears evenly dark, but in good light the dull maroon of the head and neck can be seen. Young birds are white and molt through a "calico" phase discussed on page 68.

Great Blue Heron

young

great blue

little blue

"calico" phase

Little Blue Heron

GREAT EGRET

Plume hunters destroyed entire colonies of nesting egrets at the end of the 19th century, disrupting even the nesting of species they were not hunting. Opposition to the wanton killing coalesced into the Audubon movement, which brought the era of millinery slaughter to an end.

From Florida north to South Carolina, wood storks are seen in freshwater swamps. They are large white birds with black wing markings and bare black heads.

Egret is another name for heron. The name comes from the long, showy white plumes, "aigrettes," on the backs of some herons in breeding plumage. These plumes, prized adornments for women's hats at the time, led to the birds' slaughter and near extinction a century ago.

The great egret and snowy egret (p. 70), the two most persecuted egrets, have made a comeback. Great egrets are numerous and conspicuous on freshwater marshes. They prey heavily on fish but take frogs, insects, and other prey as well. They hunt alone or in small groups, often freezing until prey appears.

The great egret is the largest white heron, but the sure marks separating it from other white herons are bill and leg color. The **great egret** has black legs and a yellow bill. A small area in front of the eyes turns bright green briefly during nesting.

Young little blue herons are white. Only the bill color, blue–gray blending to black at the tip, is the same as in the adult. The bill color and greenish yellow legs distinguish it from other white herons. There is also an inconspicuous amount of gray on the wing tips. Before turning dark, little blue herons molt through a "calico" phase—white with splotchy gray marks.

68

Young Little Blue Heron

Great Egret

WHITE HERONS

CATTLE EGRET

SNOWY EGRET

The smallest of the white egrets, the **cattle egret** also has a comparatively shorter, thicker neck and shorter bill than other slender white herons, giving it a more compact look. The bill is yellow to orange; leg color varies with season. In breeding plumage, cattle egrets show buff plumes on the crown, neck, and back.

Cattle egrets first invaded the southeastern US in the 1950s. Their remarkable colonization of North America is virtually complete, although they are still colonizing some western areas. In much of the South, cattle egrets are the most common heron. They roost and nest in wetlands but feed on insects disturbed by grazing livestock and are usually seen in pastures.

Snowy egrets, like most herons, patrol marshes and wetlands for a living. They are fairly numerous on fresh water in summer and during migration, but most winter on coasts. It is suspected that their bright yellow toes are used to attract prey. They sometimes hunt actively, even sprinting through shallows after fish.

Snowy egrets have black bills with some yellow in front of the eye. Their legs are also black, but the feet are bright yellow. "Golden slippers" is a popular name for the bird. In young birds, a yellow stripe runs from the foot up the back of the legs.

peak breeding

breeding

Cattle Egret

young

young

Snowy Egret

WHITE-FACED IBIS

GLOSSY IBIS

WHITE IBIS

Ancestors of the white-faced ibis invaded North America thousands of years ago. The glossy ibis arrived in the 1800s. Both probably evolved from the same Old World species.

bises are most notable for their long, curved bills. They feed in marshes and wetlands, even flooded lawns after a good rain. They eat almost any aquatic life they can catch, but their slim, curved bills are a special threat to burrowing crabs and snails. The tips of their bills are sensitive, and most prey is caught by probing, not by sight.

White ibis adults are boldly red and white with small black wing tips. (During nesting, the outer portion of the bill turns dark.) Young birds are brown above, but their white bellies distinguish them from other ibises. White ibises are seen on both fresh and salt water but never far from coasts. They feed in flocks, which may be large.

White-faced and **glossy ibises** are very similar birds. In fact, their winter plumages are nearly identical. Only the red eye of the adult white-faced reliably distinguishes it from the glossy ibis in winter. Ranges of the two species overlap from eastern Texas to Mississippi. In breeding plumage, the area around the eye is a good mark, but can be seen only at close range or with good binoculars. The flesh near the eye is reddish with a narrow border of white feathers in the white-faced. In the glossy ibis, the eye area is bluish with a pale blue border.

summer glossy

summer white-faced

winter

White-faced and Glossy Ibises

young

White Ibis

molting young

young

AMERICAN BITTERN

GREEN HERON

LIMPKIN

The American bittern hides by freezing in place. It stands with its neck and bill extended straight up, blending into the background reeds and even swaying with them.

itterns are members of the heron family. Limpkins are in a family of their own. **Limpkins** have down-curved bills like those of the ibises (p. 72). White streaks and spots extending from the head to the dull brown body distinguish them from any ibis. The limpkin lives in marshes, preying predominantly on a single food—the apple snail. It is best known for its loud, anguished, wailing call at night, which has earned it the name "crying bird."

The **American bittern** is also best known for its call. It is a shy marsh bird, much harder to see than a limpkin, but its call is as loud, intriguing, and improbable as the limpkin's. *"Pump-per-lunk"* is a common description, but that barely conveys the mechanical character or the drama of the sound. Sometimes seen in flight, it is distinguished from other stocky herons by the dark trailing edge of its wing.

The green heron is usually seen singly at the edge of still or slow-moving water. It often crouches quietly on limbs or vegetation closely overhanging the water's surface, waiting for small fish. No heron waits more patiently. The **green heron** is small, about the size of a crow. Its upperparts are actually blue-green. At a distance or in poor light, the bird looks dark overall except for its bright yellow or orange legs. It gives a loud *kowp!* when disturbed.

American Bittern

Green Heron

young

Limpkin

YELLOW-CROWNED NIGHT-HERON

BLACK-CROWNED NIGHT-HERON

All herons roost and nest in trees for protection from predators. The night-herons are just the most obvious in many areas because of their habit of roosting during the day.

Heron nesting colonies often include a variety of species.

The night-herons are bulky birds that often sit hunched up. They resemble the green heron and bittern in the preceding illustration much more than the slender, elegant herons at the beginning of the wading bird section.

Flocks of night-herons roost in shrubs and trees when not hunting, often in daytime. They are fairly tame and can be seen near suburbs and fishing camps. They hunt singly or in small groups, usually at dusk or even at night. The black-crowned night-heron takes a wide variety of prey and is adept at catching most, including fish. Yellow-crowns usually stalk crabs and have heavy bills for cracking the shells.

Adult night-herons have distinctly different plumages, but the brown young can be confused with each other and with the American bittern shown on the preceding page. Bill shape is a good mark separating young **yellow-crowned night-herons** from young **black-crowns.** Both birds have heavy bills, but the yellow-crown's is heavier and shorter. Young black-crowns go through several brown variations before achieving adult plumage in their third year.

In flight, the long legs of the yellow-crowned are a good mark, extending well beyond the tail. Only the feet of the black-crowned trail the tail.

Yellow-crowned
Night-heron

young

Black-crowned Night-heron

2nd year

young

BITTERN AND RAIL

LEAST BITTERN

KING RAIL

Toxic waste tends to concentrate in marshes, carried there by the steady flow of water. Marsh hens, as hunters call king and clapper rails, have such high mercury levels in some areas that hunters are advised not to eat them.

Least bitterns are rail-like members of the heron family—the smallest herons. Both they and the king rail are birds of freshwater marshes that have declined greatly in the last few decades with the loss of wetlands. Enough king rails still remain to support hunting in a number of states, but least bitterns are scarce.

Although they are sometimes seen fluttering over a marsh, least bitterns usually scamper through marsh vegetation. They can burrow through matted grasses or clamber reed to reed several feet above the ground. Fish and insects such as dragonflies are primary foods.

Least bitterns have tawny underparts. Males have black backs and crowns; females, brown. In flight, the wing patches are good marks. Calls are less distinctive than in some other marsh birds, and least bitterns give so many that it requires experience to recognize them.

The call is the best mark for the **king rail.** It gives a dry, chattering *kek-kek-kek-kek-kek* that starts slow and loud, then gradually softens while speeding up. Be sure the call comes from a freshwater marsh. The clapper rail of saltwater marshes looks much like the king rail and sounds identical. The two meet in brackish marshes. King rails feed heavily on crustaceans such as crayfish and crabs.

Least Bittern

least bittern

♂

♀

King Rail

SORA

VIRGINIA RAIL

The common expression "thin as a rail" refers to the narrow bodies of these birds. Their bodies are not only thin but flexible, so that they can squeeze through openings even narrower than the bird is wide.

Rails are shy birds that typically remain hidden in heavy marsh vegetation. They are seldom seen, although both the sora (a rail) and the Virginia rail are numerous. Flood conditions sometimes force them from cover. Rails swim, but walking is their preferred way of getting around; with their long toes, they can walk on floating vegetation. They occasionally fly, although they usually run or dive underwater when disturbed.

On their freshwater nesting marshes, the **sora** and **Virginia rail** are usually identified by their calls. Soras often give a rising *ker-wee;* when alarmed, they give a loud *keek*. The Virginia rail makes a metallic clicking sound in spring, *ti-dick, ti-dick*. Throughout the summer, they give pig-like grunts and make a sound similar to a duck's *quack*. Calls are regularly heard in winter also, but the sora and Virginia rail withdraw from most of their freshwater range in winter.

The sora and Virginia rail look plump from the side but are very thin, making it easy for them to thread through marsh tangles. The best visual marks for the sora are the short, chicken-like bill, black mask, and greenish legs. The Virginia rail suggests a scaled-down king rail (p. 78); the long, reddish bill and legs and the black-and-white flanks are good marks.

80

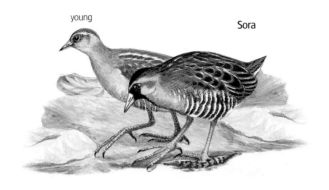

young

Sora

young

chick

Virginia Rail

STILT AND AVOCET

STILT

AVOCET

Avocets and stilts both give loud and distinctive calls when they take flight. The avocet's call is a penetrating *kleep! kleep!* Stilts give a sharp *yip-yip-yip.*

oth the **stilt** and the **avocet,** members of the same family, are striking birds that need little description beyond their illustrations. When either bird wades, the extreme length of its legs can be concealed, but in flight, the legs are seen to trail far beyond the tail. Note that the avocet loses the rusty head and neck color in winter. Sexes can be distinguished in both species. Female stilts are a bit browner above than the black-backed male. Female avocets have shorter and more sharply bent bills.

Both species are numerous in the West on shallow freshwater and alkaline lakes. They were once common in the East, but their range and numbers have diminished with loss of habitat. They sometimes share the same ponds or lakes, feeding in separate groups.

Avocets typically feed by sweeping their bills through bottom mud and catching any small prey that is disturbed. The bill tips are very sensitive to touch. When water is too deep for wading, they sometimes swim. Their feet are webbed for efficient swimming.

Stilts can swim too, but they seldom do. They usually pick insects or other tiny aquatic life from the surface of still water. Their legs are so long that, on land, they can't pick from the ground without crouching.

82

Stilt

♂

♀

Avocet

♂

summer

♀

winter

LONG-BILLED CURLEW

WHIMBREL

MARBLED GODWIT

In spring, Hudsonian godwits migrate north through Texas and the central states and provinces. They are scarce and easily distinguished from marbled godwits by their black-and-white tails

I n most inland areas, godwits and whimbrels are seen only in migration, and few whimbrels migrate inland. However, curlews nest and migrate over much of the West. They sometimes gather in large flocks during migration. Curlews are also found on freshwater in winter in a very limited range.

Size is a good first mark for godwits, curlews, and whimbrels. All are conspicuously large sandpipers. Females are slightly larger than males and have longer bills. Their plumage patterns are the mottled gray-browns typical of the entire sandpiper family.

Godwits are numerous and are seen in loose nesting colonies in the prairie pothole region. The long, upturned bill is a sure mark for the **marbled godwit** in flight as well as for standing birds. Dowitchers (p. 88) are sometimes confused with godwits but are much smaller and have straight bills.

The bills of the **whimbrel** and **long-billed curlew** are down-curved. The longer bill of the long-billed curlew is usually obvious, but some young males have bills barely larger than a whimbrel's. If in doubt, check the head for black stripes; only the whimbrel has them. In flight, the bright cinnamon on the underwings of the curlew is a good mark.

Long-billed
Curlew

Whimbrel

summer ♂

winter ♀

Marbled Godwit

WILLET AND YELLOWLEGS

LESSER YELLOWLEGS

GREATER YELLOWLEGS

WILLET

The heavy bill of the willet allows it to take larger prey than most sandpipers. Crabs are one of its favorite meals.

Yellowlegs are fairly numerous in spring and fall migration, although the lesser is scarce in the West. Willets migrate throughout the West and are fairly numerous in migration and on the wetlands where they nest. Small numbers are also seen inland in Florida.

Bright yellow legs distinguish the yellowlegs from similar birds, such as the solitary sandpiper (p. 96). Bill length and calls are the best marks separating the **greater** from the **lesser yellowlegs.** The greater's bill is half again its head length and slightly upturned; the lesser's is about the length of its head and perfectly straight. Greater yellowlegs give a ringing flight call of three to five notes; the lesser's call is flatter and one- or two-noted.

Both yellowlegs feed actively, often bobbing their heads or tails. They don't probe, but pick minnows, bugs, and other small prey from near the water's surface or at marsh edges.

Seen standing, a **willet** is a big, nondescript sandpiper with pale blue-gray legs and a dusky bill with a blue-gray base. When flushed, it reveals the dramatic white wing stripes that are its best mark. Willets nest in loose, noisy colonies, sometimes on open prairies far from water. They forage mostly in marshes and wetlands, sometimes swimming in deep marsh.

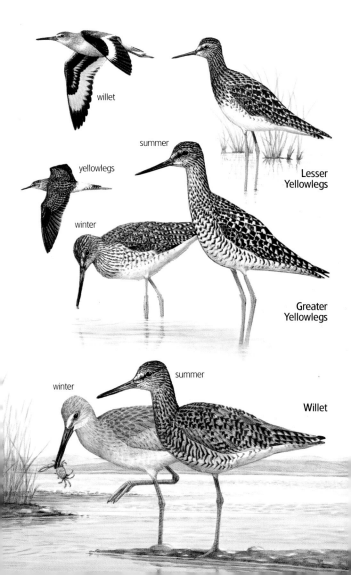

willet

yellowlegs

summer

winter

Lesser
Yellowlegs

Greater
Yellowlegs

winter

summer

Willet

DOWITCHERS

SHORT-BILLED DOWITCHER

LONG-BILLED DOWITCHER

Dowitchers are chunky sandpipers with extremely long bills. Over most of the US, they are seen on fresh water in migration. The long-billed is numerous west of the Rockies, scarce to the east, where the short-billed is the common migrating dowitcher. Both winter on coasts, but the long-billed often prefers fresh water behind the shores.

Flocks of dowitchers (sometimes mixed flocks) feed openly in shallow, muddy water. They use a rapid vertical "stitching" motion to stir up the bottom and the small aquatic life it contains. Snipe, the only similar long-billed bird (p. 90), are wary and normally solitary.

Besides their long bills, dowitchers show a distinctive white wedge on their backs and rumps in flight. Bill length is not a reliable mark separating **short-billed dowitchers** from **long-bills;** flight calls are. Short-bills give a mellow *tu-tu-tu;* long-bills, a thin, high-pitched *keek*.

In winter, even experts can seldom separate the two dowitchers by plumage in the field. They do better in summer, but three races of the short-billed, all with their own slight plumage variations, make for one of birding's most challenging identification problems. Fortunately, the birds announce who they are with their flight calls when they take off.

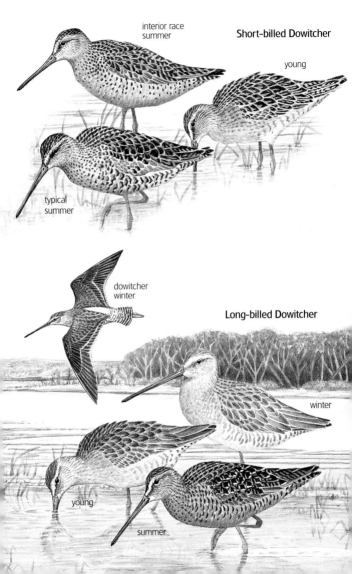

interior race
summer

Short-billed Dowitcher

young

typical
summer

dowitcher
winter

Long-billed Dowitcher

winter

young

summer

SNIPE AND SANDPIPERS

RUDDY TURNSTONE

BUFF-BREASTED SANDPIPER

SNIPE

More snipe may have been shot than any other gamebird. Yet they still thrive because of their wariness. The relatively tame buff-breasted sandpipers were nearly extirpated.

Turnstones are numerous on beaches and mudflats during migration, usually in small flocks. They use their short, slightly up-turned bills to flip pebbles and root through sand and vegetation for food. **Ruddy turn-stones** are one of the most distinctive and dramatically plumaged shorebirds.

Buff-breasted sandpipers are scarce migrants. They favor short grass—pastures, wetland margins, sod farms—and often stop at the same sites yearly. Like the plovers that follow, buff-breasted sandpipers pick food from the ground's surface rather than probing beneath. Fall migration is broader than mapped, extending from British Columbia to Nova Scotia. The breast color is a good mark for the **buff-breasted sandpiper;** the clincher is the bright contrast of the white underwing in flight.

Snipe seldom reveal themselves on beaches or shores but feed alone and secretively, often at dusk or dawn, in bogs, marshes, and wet grass. They plunge their long bills into soft earth and feel for prey with the sensitive bill tip.

Their long bills distinguish **snipe** from all but the dowitchers, which lack the snipe's bold head stripes. When disturbed, snipe take off in zigzag flight with a loud *scaip* call. They are fairly numerous but declining in the East.

summer

Ruddy Turnstone

winter

**Buff-breasted
Sandpiper**

Snipe

PLOVERS

KILLDEER

AMERICAN GOLDEN-PLOVER

BLACK-BELLIED PLOVER

Plovers often range farther from water than sandpipers. Because they pick from the ground's surface, they can find food on hard, dry land.

lovers are different from sandpipers. They have distinctive bills—pigeon-like, short, and slightly swollen at the tip. They feed in a distinctive stop-and-go fashion, sprinting a short distance and abruptly pausing to pick at food, then looking about and dashing off again. They don't probe into the ground as sandpipers do, but pick food from the surface.

The two black neck bands are sure marks for one species of plover, the **killdeer**. In flight, the orange back and rump are obvious. Killdeer are numerous and widespread (usually alone or in small groups) in open areas from shores to bare or short-grass fields distant from water.

We are treated to the **American golden-plover's** singular gold-flecked beauty only during spring migration over the central continent. They are numerous, found on habitats like those used by killdeer. Fall migration is largely off the Atlantic coast.

Black-bellied plovers in their striking breeding plumage are found on freshwater borders during spring migration. Some also use fields and rain-flooded pastures for stopovers. In fall and winter, the plumage is pale gray, with dark eyes, bill, and legs providing sharp contrast. A good mark year-round is the black "wingpit" seen in flight.

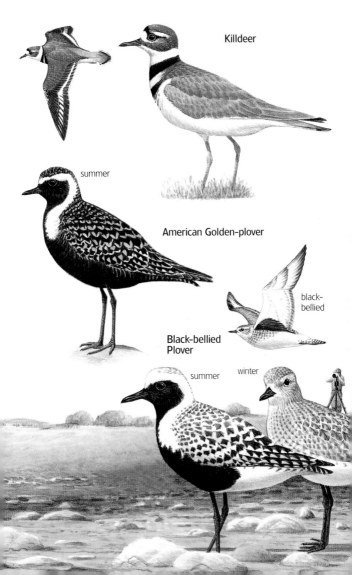

Killdeer

summer

American Golden-plover

black-bellied

Black-bellied Plover

summer   winter

PLOVERS

SNOWY PLOVER

PIPING PLOVER

SEMIPALMATED PLOVER

The small plovers, except for the semi-palmated, are rare and declining. They are disappearing because the sand flats and beaches that they use for feeding and nesting are the same ones people use for recreation. The semipalmated is not threatened because it nests safely in the remote Arctic.

Only about 1,500 pairs of piping plovers nest on freshwater beaches and sandbars (about 25 pairs on the Great Lakes). Some beaches are reserved and protected for their nesting in order to stave off extinction. Their pale backs blend so well into the dry sand background that **piping plovers** are hard to locate even when present. Note the stubby bill and orange legs. The black neck band can be incomplete.

The legs are black and the bill thinner on **snowy plovers.** Their populations are not in much better shape than the piping plover's. Only around 20,000 birds survive in the US.

The **semipalmated plover,** the darkest of the three small plovers, is often seen on wet sand or mudflats. It most resembles the piping plover with its orange legs and bicolored bill in summer. The best marks, other than the wet-sand back color, are the black face markings. Flocks of semipalmated plovers are fairly numerous on fresh water during migration.

snowy

piping

semipalmated

Snowy Plover

summer

winter

Piping Plover

winter

summer

Semipalmated Plover

winter

summer

young

SANDPIPERS

SOLITARY SANDPIPER

SPOTTED SANDPIPER

Spotted sandpipers reverse the typical sex roles of shorebirds (and humans). Females are the aggressors; males raise the young.

Females arrive first on the nesting ground. After attracting a mate and laying eggs, the female often lets the male care for the nest while she nests again with other males.

Solitary and spotted sandpipers are usually seen singly, sometimes in pairs, rarely in small groups. Even during migration, when many shorebirds are noted for their large concentrations, these two go it alone.

Both are widespread and adaptable. A sandpiper seen alone where you might not expect one could well be a spotted or solitary sandpiper. Other sandpipers seldom visit forest lakes, drainage ditches, or park ponds.

Across most of the US, **solitary sandpipers** are seen during migration. They have no immediately obvious plumage marks (which, in itself, is a useful mark). Their plumage and shape suggest a small yellowlegs (p. 86), but note the gray legs. The thin white eye-ring and black tail bands are also useful marks. More obvious are its head-bobbing habit and its practice of stretching its wings high after landing, exposing the dark undersides, before slowly folding them.

The teetering walk of the **spotted sandpiper** is usually the first mark noted. In summer, the spotted breast is a sure mark. In winter, note the thin white wedge in front of the folded wing. Spotted sandpipers fly close to the water, typically going only a short distance before returning to shore. They glide on bowed, quivering wings interrupted by shallow, stiff wingbeats.

96

Solitary Sandpiper

solitary

spotted

Spotted Sandpiper

winter

summer

DUNLIN

WILSON'S PHALAROPE

STILT SANDPIPER

In fall, some red-necked phalaropes migrate through the West. Their thin bills are shorter than Wilson's.

Sex roles are reversed in phalaropes, as in the spotted sandpiper (see sidebar, p. 96).

Wilson's phalarope is fairly numerous in summer and during migration in western shallow wetlands. It is scarce in the East. After nesting, the birds gather in large numbers at a few salty inland lakes (half a million at Great Salt Lake, UT) before flying south.

The best mark for **Wilson's phalarope** is the long, thin bill—longer than that of the lesser yellowlegs (p. 86), thinner than the greater yellowlegs'. In flight, the white rump is a helpful mark. Females are more colorful than males.

The dunlin and stilt sandpiper are fairly numerous and widespread inland during migration. In spring, the black belly patch of the **dunlin** and the extensive black barring on the underparts of the **stilt sandpiper** are easy marks. The relatively long, drooped bills are sure year-round marks distinguishing the two from other small sandpipers, while the stout shape and black legs of the smaller dunlin separate it from the slender, greenish-legged stilt sandpiper. The legs can cause the stilt sandpiper to be confused with the lesser yellowlegs (p. 86), but note the bill shape and the dowitcher-like feeding style.

In flight, the stilt sandpiper resembles Wilson's phalarope, with a white rump and plain, dark wings. The dunlin has a dark center tail stripe and a white wing stripe.

winter

Dunlin

summer

dunlin

winter

summer ♀

Wilson's Phalarope

summer ♂

Wilson's
phalarope

young

stilt
sandpiper

summer

winter

Stilt Sandpiper

SANDPIPERS

PECTORAL SANDPIPER

WHITE-RUMPED SANDPIPER

BAIRD'S SANDPIPER

Sanderlings are scarce inland migrants except on the Great Lakes. Barely larger than a peep, they have a reddish breast and upperparts in spring. In fall, they are paler than the western sandpiper (p. 102).

aird's, white-rumped, and pectoral sandpipers spend much of their lives migrating between their High Arctic nesting grounds and their winter range in the most distant parts of South America. They are generally scarce, and the white-rumped is absent inland in fall, migrating off the Atlantic coast.

The sure mark for the **pectoral sandpiper** is the way the breast streaks end in a sharp line just above the white belly. There is little white in their tails. They are often seen singly among flocks of other small shorebirds. Their spring migration is heaviest in the Mississippi Valley.

Small sandpipers with white rumps, other than the **white-rumped sandpiper,** have long legs that extend behind the tail during flight (see preceding page). Like Baird's sandpiper, the white-rumped has long, slender wings. Although not obvious in flight, the wings extend visibly beyond the tail on a standing bird.

Baird's sandpipers stop in dry grassy areas as well as wetlands. They typically migrate in small groups with other small shorebirds but usually feed by themselves. Although subtle, the long wings are the best mark separating Baird's from other small sandpipers. Only the white-rumped sandpiper has a similar wing extension. Baird's rump has a black median.

young

Pectoral Sandpiper

White-rumped Sandpiper

perctoral

young

summer

white-rumped

Baird's

young

summer

Baird's Sandpiper

SANDPIPERS

SEMIPALMATED SANDPIPER

WESTERN SANDPIPER

LEAST SANDPIPER

Flight calls can be used to separate western from semi-palmated sandpipers. Semi-palms give a single short *cherk* note. Westerns give a squeaky *chir-eep*.

emipalmated, western, and least sand-pipers are often lumped together as "peeps." Baird's and white-rumped sandpipers (preceding page) are usually included in the group. Some people don't attempt to identify peeps to species, and sometimes it isn't easy or even possible. Usually, however, they can be named if you know what to look for.

Semipalmated and **western sandpipers** are hardest to separate. During fall migration, they often stump the experts. Both are gray above, white below, and have a black bill and legs. The longer bill of the western seen in the illustration is not a sure mark; bill length varies. During spring migration, the western shows a bit of rusty color on the head and wing area; it is duller or absent in the semipalmated. The streaks on the western's breast are more pronounced. They tend to extend onto the flanks and are shaped like tiny chevrons.

The least sandpiper is numerous but less so than semipalmateds and westerns. It is the only peep normally seen inland in winter. Size is a good mark. The **least** is the smallest sandpiper in the world. It is browner than other peeps (in fall and winter, compare the brown breast with the plain breast of the western), has the smallest bill, and has yellow-green (not black) legs. Beware: muddy legs can look dark.

western or
semipalmated
(winter)

summer

**Semipalmated
Sandpiper**

least
(winter)

winter

summer

**Western
Sandpiper**

winter

young

**Least
Sandpiper**

summer

DIPPER

**BELTED
KINGFISHER**

The green kingfisher is fairly numerous along the Rio Grande in southern Texas and can be found inland to the Edwards Plateau.

Green kingfishers are about the size of a starling and have green backs and crests. Males have a rusty breast band.

There are two inland waterbirds that feed like no others, the dipper and the king-fisher. Kingfishers plunge–dive for fish like terns. Unlike terns and the other plunge-diving aerialists, however, kingfishers do not spend long hours on the wing searching for prey. They perch on a limb or wire near water and wait for fish to come to them. Kingfishers often hover over suspected prey, waiting for the right moment to plunge.

As one would expect from its unique foraging style, the **belted kingfisher** looks quite differ-ent than other waterbirds. Note the large head and bill and the thick crest. Females have a rusty breast-band lacking in males. Kingfishers are noisy and conspicuous. They are fairly nu-merous and widespread at any body of water that boasts fish and a perching spot.

There are other small, nondescript, gray birds, but none with the habits of the **dipper.** They live at the side of small rushing streams, typi-cally cascading mountain flows. Amazingly, they feed on the stream bottoms, under the turbulent water, taking aquatic insects and other small organisms. It is always a surprise to see one disappear into white–water torrents. When disturbed, a dipper flies upstream or down, never away from water. Its name comes from its habitual bobbing (dipping) motion.

104

Dipper

Belted Kingfisher

♀ ♂

ow many species of birds have you identified? Keeping a record is the only way to know. Sooner or later, even the most casual bird-watcher makes notes of the species seen on a trip or in a day. People keep backyard lists, year lists, state lists, every kind of checklist. All serious birders maintain a life list. Seeing your life list grow can become part of the pleasure of bird-watching. The pages that follow are designed to serve as your checklist of freshwater waterbirds as well as an index to their illustrations in this guide.

English names listed in the index are the familiar names used in common conversation. For the most part, they are the same as the formal English names adopted by the American Ornithologists' Union in the seventh edition of their *Check-list of North American Birds,* 1998. When the formal AOU English name differs from the common name used in this guide, the AOU English name is given on the second line of the index entry. The Latin names in italics are the AOU's scientific names.

✓ Species	Date	Location
○ **A**NHINGA *Anhinga anhinga*	32	
○ **A**VOCET American Avocet *Recurvirostra americana*	82	
○ AMERICAN **B**ITTERN *Botaurus lentiginosus*	74	
○ LEAST **B**ITTERN *Ixobrychus exilis*	78	
○ **B**UFFLEHEAD *Bucephala albeola*	54	

✓	Species	Date	Location

○ **C**ANVASBACK 50
Aythya valisineria

○ **C**OOT 62
American Coot
Fulica americana

○ DOUBLE–CRESTED **C**ORMORANT 32
Phalacrocorax auritus

○ SANDHILL **C**RANE 64
Grus canadensis

○ LONG–BILLED **C**URLEW 84
Numenius americanus

○ **D**IPPER 104
American Dipper
Cinclus mexicanus

○ LONG–BILLED **D**OWITCHER 88
Limnodromus scolopaceus

○ SHORT–BILLED **D**OWITCHER 88
Limnodromus griseus

○ BLACK **D**UCK 40
American Black Duck
Anas rubripes

○ MOTTLED **D**UCK 40
Anas fulvigula

○ RING–NECKED **D**UCK 48
Aythya collaris

○ RUDDY **D**UCK 50
Oxyura jamaicensis

○ WOOD **D**UCK 38
Aix sponsa

○ **D**UNLIN 98
Calidris alpina

○ CATTLE **E**GRET 70
Bubulcus ibis

○ GREAT **E**GRET 68
Ardea alba

✓ Species		Date	Location
◯ SNOWY **E**GRET *Egretta thula*	70		
◯ **G**ADWALL *Anas strepera*	42		
◯ PURPLE **G**ALLINULE *Porphyrula martinica*	62		
◯ MARBLED **G**ODWIT *Limosa fedoa*	84		
◯ AMERICAN **G**OLDEN-PLOVER *Pluvialis dominica*	92		
◯ BARROW'S **G**OLDENEYE *Bucephala islandica*	52		
◯ COMMON **G**OLDENEYE *Bucephala clangula*	52		
◯ CANADA **G**OOSE *Branta canadensis*	34		
◯ ROSS' **G**OOSE Ross's Goose *Chen rossii*	36		
◯ SNOW **G**OOSE *Chen caerulescens*	36		
◯ WHITE-FRONTED **G**OOSE Greater White-fronted Goose *Anser albifrons*	34		
◯ CLARK'S **G**REBE *Aechmophorus clarkii*	58		
◯ EARED **G**REBE *Podiceps nigricollis*	60		
◯ HORNED **G**REBE *Podiceps auritus*	60		
◯ PIED-BILLED **G**REBE *Podilymbus podiceps*	58		
◯ RED-NECKED **G**REBE *Podiceps grisegena*	60		

✓ Species		Date	Location

◯ WESTERN **G**REBE   58
Aechmophorus occidentalis

◯ BONAPARTE'S **G**ULL   20
Larus philadelphia

◯ CALIFORNIA **G**ULL   18
Larus californicus

◯ FRANKLIN'S **G**ULL   20
Larus pipixcan

◯ HERRING **G**ULL   18
Larus argentatus

◯ RING-BILLED **G**ULL   20
Larus delawarensis

◯ GREAT BLUE **H**ERON   66
Ardea herodias

◯ GREEN **H**ERON   74
Butorides virescens

◯ LITTLE BLUE **H**ERON   66
Egretta caerulea

◯ GLOSSY **I**BIS   72
Plegadis falcinellus

◯ WHITE **I**BIS   72
Eudocimus albus

◯ WHITE-FACED **I**BIS   72
Plegadis chihi

◯ **K**ILLDEER   92
Charadrius vociferus

◯ BELTED **K**INGFISHER   104
Ceryle alcyon

◯ **L**IMPKIN   74
Aramus guarauna

◯ COMMON **L**OON   30
Gavia immer

◯ **M**ALLARD   40
Anas platyrhynchos

✓ Species		Date	Location

COMMON **M**ERGANSER 56
Mergus merganser

HOODED **M**ERGANSER 54
Lophodytes cucullatus

RED–BREASTED **M**ERGANSER 56
Mergus serrator

MOORHEN 62
Common Moorhen
Gallinula chloropus

BLACK–CROWNED **N**IGHT–HERON 76
Nycticorax nycticorax

YELLOW–CROWNED **N**IGHT–HERON 76
Nyctanassa violacea

WHITE **P**ELICAN 30
American White Pelican
Pelecanus erythrorhynchos

WILSON'S **P**HALAROPE 98
Phalaropus tricolor

PINTAIL 42
Northern Pintail
Anas acuta

BLACK–BELLIED **P**LOVER 92
Pluvialis squatarola

PIPING **P**LOVER 94
Charadrius melodus

SEMIPALMATED **P**LOVER 94
Charadrius semipalmatus

SNOWY **P**LOVER 94
Charadrius alexandrinus

KING **R**AIL 78
Rallus elegans

VIRGINIA **R**AIL 80
Rallus limicola

REDHEAD 50
Aythya americana

✓ Species	Date	Location

○ BAIRD'S **S**ANDPIPER   100
Calidris bairdii

○ BUFF−BREASTED **S**ANDPIPER   90
Tryngites subruficollis

○ LEAST **S**ANDPIPER   102
Calidris minutilla

○ PECTORAL **S**ANDPIPER   100
Calidris melanotos

○ SEMIPALMATED **S**ANDPIPER   102
Calidris pusilla

○ SOLITARY **S**ANDPIPER   96
Tringa solitaria

○ SPOTTED **S**ANDPIPER   96
Actitis macularia

○ STILT **S**ANDPIPER   98
Calidris himantopus

○ WESTERN **S**ANDPIPER   102
Calidris mauri

○ WHITE−RUMPED **S**ANDPIPER   100
Calidris fuscicollis

○ LESSER **S**CAUP   48
Aythya affinis

○ **S**HOVELER   44
Northern Shoveler
Anas clypeata

○ **S**NIPE   90
Common Snipe
Gallinago gallinago

○ **S**ORA   80
Porzana carolina

○ **S**TILT   82
Black-necked Stilt
Himantopus mexicanus

○ MUTE **S**WAN   28
Cygnus olor

✓ Species	Date	Location
○ TRUMPETER SWAN *Cygnus buccinator*	28	
○ TUNDRA SWAN *Cygnus columbianus*	28	
○ BLUE–WINGED TEAL *Anas discors*	46	
○ CINNAMON TEAL *Anas cyanoptera*	46	
○ GREEN–WINGED TEAL *Anas crecca*	46	
○ BLACK TERN *Chlidonias niger*	24	
○ CASPIAN TERN *Sterna caspia*	24	
○ COMMON TERN *Sterna hirundo*	26	
○ FORSTER'S TERN *Sterna forsteri*	26	
○ LEAST TERN *Sterna antillarum*	24	
○ RUDDY TURNSTONE *Arenaria interpres*	90	
○ GREATER YELLOWLEGS *Tringa melanoleuca*	86	
○ LESSER YELLOWLEGS *Tringa flavipes*	86	
○ WHIMBREL *Numenius phaeopus*	84	
○ FULVOUS WHISTLING-DUCK *Dendrocygna bicolor*	38	
○ AMERICAN WIGEON *Anas americana*	44	
○ WILLET *Catoptrophorus semipalmatus*	86	